THIS IS THE LAST TIME

# this is the last time

poems by

## chris taylor

OUTPOST PRESS
ABIQUIU, NEW MEXICO

All Rights Reserved
Published in 2024 by Outpost Press
An imprint of Wayfarer Books
Cover Design and Interior Design by Connor Wolfe
TRADE PAPERBACK 978-1-965320-38-9

10 9 8 7 6 5 4 3 2 1

Look for our titles in paperback, ebook, and audiobook wherever books are sold.
Wholesale offerings for retailers available through Ingram.

Outpost Press is committed to ecological stewardship.
We greatly value the natural environment and invest in conservation.

PO Box 1109, Abiquiú, NM 87510-1109

413.441.7003 | orders@homeboundpublications.com

WAYFARERBOOKS.ORG

# Acknowledgments

"halloween costume" is published on *Teen Ink*

poems "pink" and "who am i" is published *POETiCA Review,* Summer 2024

"leaf lace" will be published in the October 2024 issue of *Audience Askew*

"coffee breath" is included in Creative Communications' Summer 2024 anthology for young writers

"poorly kept" is included in *American High School Poets Summer 2024 Anthology* from justpoetry.org

# contents

**One: hoard**

3      pink

5      mars

6      the quiet kid

7      am i self-absorbed?

8      ceramicist

9      candlestick

10      coffee breath

11      extract

12      me when

13      stomach acid

14      wire sand

16      fireworks come at the end

17      spicy food

18      tolerance

19      tumor

21      her favorite movie applies

22      pressed flower

23      spores

## Two: Heard

27     leaf lace

28     balcony song

29     i've always written

30     medieval cat painting

31     late apology

32     painter tape

33     halloween costume

34     peach

35     rest

36     plexiglass

38     ode (?) to my door

39     talking about me

41     who am i

42     laced up

43     unflavored addiction

44     puddles

45     making vows

47     ambulance

48     one what i share with you

49     doubt

51     helium

52     eavesdropping on

53     poorly kept

# ONE

# hoard

# pink

he said he found it there,
that pink chemical filled with power,
tiny lethality in his hand,
he found it and lost it, in the trees he said,
where someone else might find death,

then maybe i am a
dog tied to a tree, tight on my leash, i smell it,
the bright pigmented seed had bloomed already
into a flower with such intensely sweet perfume
it drags me closer by my nose,

the scent excites me so
i bark and all the animals gather round
and fight for the color, so enticing,
they pass away trying to die in a way
that would make their friends proud,

but as i still survive,
the last dog in that pack of hungry beasts,
i could feast on my victory
and leave, swallow the petals the pollen the stem
and the seed that started it all,

"to hesitate is weak,"
i say to my strong self
as i hesitate day after day,
see the pink melt and fill the air with a haze

that might have been poison,
my owner would have said,
"flowers aren't for eating,"
i argue this isn't entirely true,
i've been in the forest so long, colors are my friend, and what prettier
shade exists than those glorious beings?

thinking of owner,
their soft voice and clear words,
they love the color pink,
but not in flowers, only in their clothes,
so people acknowledge them as a deeper person too,

but me, nothing but a dog in the forest,
nothing but a creature who'd fucked up
wishing for life to be more,
i have space in my lungs for every speck of pink air, i think, my
stomach could handle one flower,
but i can eat it a hundred times and still be here.

# Mars

It's lonely here, red deserts of rust,
I want help, for someone to come to my rescue,
With dune buggies, camels,
Fit for two,
They will find lone mattress in dust;
Me forever defenseless,
Observing,
Can't tell what stains are dirt from what stains are blood.

Mars gave me formidable armor,
It won't stop the sand from seeping into my clothes,
Filling my eyes, mouth,
The holes that let me breathe.
Even as the armor calms the war,
It melts and I know
It was in my lungs the whole time, still I am far from life.

# the quiet kid

if anyone finds me before i fade
out, remember my face wasn't real,
my opinions were lies, i only ever
copied you, assumed you wanted to hear my
ugly voice.

allow me, i will be your doormat,
tell me the truth. tell me i should be
seen and not heard, i'm begging you
to reinforce my roaring thoughts, to justify my
underlying silence

we can go, together, home to where
i laid rose petals on the California king, i
will help you stitch my mouth shut in the most
romantic way, bring us close, once and for all, my
voice will stop.

i salute you when you give commands,
your words will tweak the plans i made to
speak my mind, i find when i invent new sentences
and bad excuses they come out wrong and it's just
another scratch in my tongue,

keep tightening your grip on my vocal
chords, bruised and sore from spoken poetry
that lacks authenticity, i choke. i choke on your
deceptions, your deceit has always been my favorite
dinner, but this time i'll cough it up

# am i self-absorbed?

i read faces so i know you're mad
i say sorry again
and again
until i can't

Socrates, "we are what we
repeatedly do" i am a mistake
far too conceited to be human
vainglorious, complacent

unchangeable, deranged in a monster
mask, i blather on and break things
a snake mindlessly constricting and
slithering to the next victim

i keep draining my feelings dry, prying
open skin, porous, leaking endless error
i am terrified but i still ask
despite my fear, my tears, i scream

do gods account for your intentions
when they decide your end?
does taking more than i needed
mean i'll be sent away in death?

# ceramicist

i paint my skin with clay
i shape my body
to create the perfect
person

with shoulders telling
you i'm sick
i carve the curves
i stain the lips
hoping the lavender
smells like me
i take away its life
and the clay dries

into greenware, into the kiln
the burning feeling of fulfillment
till i'm just cured enough
to stand still in the studio

bone dry life sized figurine
hollowed out
glazed in cum and
blood and tears

the painter is unknown to me
puts me on
display for the disturbed
with frozen porcelain glossy face
ashamed of how i made me

# candlestick

observe the strangers in your row,
the other candles' flames,
something,
anything,
noticing everything,
find what you did wrong,
erase your place on the bench,
trade your words as wicks
and wait,
befriend
the desperation
of awaiting disappointment,
pass the candle to your left,
don't be the one to spill.
wax on your skirt?
that's not
normal.

so you spill it, spill the candlestick,
walk along the pew of judges,
drip the wax on the laps
of
people
who
don't
know
you
exist.

# coffee breath

Coffee on my shirt,
Pearls of liquid tumble down,
My hair sticks to my neck,
I smell my own spit and am disgusted how it tastes
So I hold my breath and sit,
Wearing a mask to hide my guilty mouth and pimples on my chin,

Coffee smells stronger
Than my love for unknown things,
Pour fear into the cup
And drink and drink, burp the air received as I
Chug and guzzle down each mug,
Forever this is all I eat, it's dark, stains my lips, my clothes,

I want to bathe in
Sweet-smelling, bitter-tasting
Cold brew, attracting flies,
Moldy when that last sip remains at the bottom
For days while I fall asleep,
Caffeine infecting me, crashing energy again and again,

No spoons left to stir
The thick foam into the thin body
When I brew my thousandth
Eight-ounce serving, sweating, saying all
The wrongs I've committed
Are side effects of over-consuming
Coffee.

# extract

you bought childhood,
playful remnants of the time before,
take it,
put it in a pan with
half a cup of water,
boil, stirring constantly
then bring it to a simmer,

breathe the steam,
you're not allowed to eat it anymore,
unsure
exactly what the scent is,
unable to place it,
but it stings your lonely nostrils
like cleaning chemicals,

cooked, drizzled
with a glaze of your depression's extract,
plated
nicely, on the finest china,
a single serving served
to famously hateful critics
with unresponsive faces,

they eat it
with their hands, loud, disgusting, chewing,
mocking,
licking long and slimy fingers
before they lean over
to throw it back up on the floor,
forcing you to clean it

# me when

A sinkhole opens often in my throat,
A vacuum claiming it's about to take my larynx,
To leave a place where beautiful things can grow,
Replace these unstable words
Of hate and love, out of control sentences,

Knowing my speech could be gone any second,
Speak words, nonsense, louder than I knew I could,
Get it all out before it dies, expecting, but,
My voice remains, keeps talking,
Me when, me, me when, me when, me, me,

Tears come with fearful speech but my tone is calm,
You didn't ask, I'll shut up now, no I won't.
What penalty will I get today, bruises, sickness, cuts?
I could smother myself with a pillow,
Maybe tear out my automatic tongue,
Stop talking, Dead.

# stomach acid

i feel it, it's there! it's as if i reached
my hand deep into the toilet after use
to retrieve the guts i spilled,
i pushed too hard, and
when i stood up, looking down into the bowl,
crimson red, sacks of blood just sitting there,
spreading through water, eating itself, sprouting, flowering,

then relaxing as my fingers go in
there, eyes closed, disturb it with intention,
with no sound, what a feeling!
slime, flesh, water. dirt,
won't wash off my skin, inciting criticism,
adding insecurity after insecurity,
i can't touch anything else until it leaves.

my hands tainted, permanently scarlet,
pink, glossy like they never left the bathroom.
years later now, and my hands
and arms are as clean
as i could get them. scrubbed my body red and raw,
something only i see won't go away unless i lose my eyes.

# wire sand

to bend a wire is to work a certain muscle rarely seen,
stretching your skin,
engraving metal dust in the tips of your fingers,
pliers aren't quite strong enough to shape it how you want.
beach days, frequently, nearly too much to keep up,
but, your wire cutters work on anything.
broken things can't break anymore,
now, they can only fix,
right? only improves if it can't get worse,
twist it into the shape of the pit of a peach,
an eye,
but never a form the crystal fits.

maybe you should buy a rock with sharp, jagged edges,
so it latches on
and stays together when you lose it in the swimming pond,
notice, but it's too far gone, and your suit is worn down,
you could retrieve it anyway, but your chest is exposed,
you refuse to enter the water naked
for fear of the rumored leeches,
snakes, and monster seaweed,
sickness, bacteria, porta-potty-blue streaks
an infection that threatens the deeper you sink,
but you
don't have a thing for them, you just want your pendant, back

to the car, dripping wet, sitting down in a towel,
staining everything,

rich with that pondwater smell, blue, dirty, lacking jewelry,
bare with pond-hair, pond-feet, sand in every crevice,
never want to see the beach again, although you have to
if you want to be accepted,
if you want to have your necklace back,
no one else cares how deep
but you, don't slam the door yet, get back on that raft!
this crowd can't complain about your lack of swimsuit,
don't you
want that precious stone back?

# fireworks come at the end

this is my festival of mistakes,
erasers dragging across keloids, scraping
over bedrock, heavy lead parasites
dismembered by its mass.

coffee stain under white shimmering lines
enclosed in rusted flesh, steaming,
i boiled it in the microwave. i'll press skin
against skin and burn away the first

layer, the second, then the hardwood
floors, cringe at the pain but the
ceaseless words: it's okay because you
deserve it, drip repeatedly from

broken lighters. i can't not listen. in
a billion years or so it will say
something worthwhile, and start
the fire i've been failing to feed for weeks.

it will take a break from crackling
and flare.

# spicy food

can i just take a second
for soliloquy? because
i am embarrassed
at the moment. red face
blushed and holding

back dissent, i don't know
what it will look like
coming out. the inside
of my mouth feels red
because i gorge chili

peppers when ashamed.
what if, what if i choke
on this? shrieking, weeping
from throat obstruction,
molten iron scooped from

hell, the opposite of
ice cream. that's the
chaser to my guilt
before bed, the vultures
out at night are going to

keep me up anyway.
goodnight, crimson sky.
i will see you in a
few short minutes.

# tolerance

i am your next sacrifice,
i can wash your feet,
can feed you the finest meat and rice,
tell you stories,
you as the hero,
me as the villain who falls for you.

in your glass secluded house,
i sense exposure,
even when there's no one here to see
as i tend to you,
poison in your bread,
baked from scratch, little more each slice,

a tolerance so that one day,
if i change my mind
and try to get rid of you, i can't.
i wait with patience,
i'm not allowed to
make myself immune to sodium, suffocation, guns.

as much as i pray for life,
this is all i have,
i enjoy it until you get mad.
run a bubble bath,
you oversized child,
i'll be here every day til you say it's my last

# tumor

undiagnosed.
what carcinogen did i consume?
what made the turning point,
how could i have known?

it was just there,
infinitesimal, just below
my heart, rate slowed at every
minute growth spurt,

it feeds on me,
weeks on end of seething, not speaking,
just watching the world,
passive around me,

then the first mouth,
initially obscured, but now a
tooth, then more, observed
emerging from the mound,

spouting new sounds,
yelling out to those outside, they're lies,
listeners don't know
my lips didn't procure them,

once it gains gums,
canines, begins to eat organ walls,
flesh digesting in its newly formed
miniature stomach,

follicles, hair,
tied snugly, obstructing aorta,
the abomination uses it
as a straw to drink my life,

as a tumor,
it loves more than ever, more than others,
ever-growing being, teratoma,
tortured long as it's trapped in me,

doctors don't see
the weight clearly disordered eating,
imagine their surprise when they find it!
unbeatable by surgery,
too stuck to my being, still
growing even after i'm gone.

# her favorite movie applies

my body a vessel holding passengers
each with their own story,
sprouted from a lie.
Titanic, sinking, hit an iceberg
of exposure, one slip up over thousands more,
each creation quivering, fighting to stay above
the frigid freezer-burnt water's pull,
each person waving at the sirens and
flashing lights, shrieking,
"I EXIST!"

lighthouse on a rescue boat growing closer,
bigger in perspective,
further to the dead,
they counted heads floating, motion among slabs
of ice, someone to save only showed its face
floating on a door, sending up flares, standing,
calling out conspicuously, when asked,
would only state an obvious lie
that nobody denied:
"it's a little warm."

# pressed flower

demanding,
subtle, kind,
screaming red light,
voices boiled down
to soggy spinach leaves that
still own inaudible tongues,

gentle words,
bald and tall,
accented with dead-flower
tones, hue breakable
enough, just
out of his sandpaper reach,

helping hands,
always offering,
aid not prompted, implied,
he wants something,
water into the book-vase,
never seeing his face, and

sure, he knows,
i'm not supposed to
be fed, condoned,
my bones a stem of these
dry petals, colorless,
won't give him a response.

# spores

the shower is an opposing force,
repels my dusty skin,
after all, i am the one spreading the mold,
steaming my body, turning my grey potato flakes
into thick plaque, a perfect place
for dormant spores to wake up,

i can't step foot in the tub again, not now,
not after i filled it
with all bodily fluid thought legal,
i just sat down then, in my own filth on the ceramic,
boiling water, hating myself, knowing i'm dead in
every other universe,

now all i can do is lie, lay on the bath mat,
stare at the sign on off-
white backdrop, "keep going," twisting my ribs back
and forth and back and forth, they grew sorer as they broke,
splatter everything out, bones falling through my mouth,
vomiting dirt to feed something lighter.

## TWO

# heard

# leaf lace

we used to search the autumn ground
for skeleton-like leaves,
fascinated that flesh could be
hollowed out so precisely.

i wanted to be a lacy plant,
a perfectly pristine
doily, dining with queens, blushing my
non-existent cheeks,

with burnt sienna veins, bloodless and dry,
pay it no mind, i don't
need a color, my identity doesn't have to
be anything but mine.

gradually, every bit of body, carved away,
to leave a structure,
missing everything but walls, a fragile paper,
easily destroyed.

i am the skeleton leaf, sought after,
stepped on daily,
unnoticed until you seek it, until you want it, and
forgotten when it crumbles in your hands.

# balcony song

the burning enhancing even after scalding iron is
removed, shakes you from the arm out, shivers
hot, cold, black, an overlay of verses, left me
with teardrop scars. the dog stares, no thoughts
from lonely sleepers, peace-spined, with downcast
eyes, he only burns when i'm not home, he only
shakes when doors close. suicide seems
just as harrowing as branded bodies when he

stops responding, and who says i can't spin around
and set myself on fire 'til i'm punk? undo all the
damage done by blood and replace it with sick
blisters and old plasters, that heroin slimness,
please. i don't care anymore if he watches from
a balcony. and after all the speculation, Juliet
was made to die, her verse was made to butcher.

# i've always written

it got worse over years of making my hand sore,
years of wanting to be better, or at least
be recognized,
but i made my world from words that will never make sense,
so full of desire to be different,
trying so hard, stumbling down the same stairs again,
jumping, falling, all
because i saw in a dream that i could fly,
it didn't matter if i'd also seen that i could die,
that i could mutilate my fingers, that i could down
a bottle of melatonin
gummies, take a long sleep, they said "dream big," right?

if it was real lead, i think i'd have enough to be fatal,
if a pencil is harmless in your eyes, i'll
take your leftovers,
craft a poem, season it with tablespoons of regret,
i can be creative, i can be unique, all right, you'll see,
i'm not a gift, nor gifted, i'm the one receiving unsolicited
rewards for nothing,
you read my letter, my masterpiece,
practiced my whole life for this work of art to reach you,
the most meaning i could have poured into my boiling pot of writing,
the very opposite of spoken language,
bound to be consumed through tears that may
or may not drip down your cheeks,
but i didn't mean for you to cry like that.

# medieval cat painting

she has smelled every scent that walked by,
each unshaven man, every band of jesters,
accused witches that fell apart, rejected by the monarch,

cat-human face unfit for its body, uncanny valley
appears again, chastised and shamed,
placed beneath the chopping block to watch the heads roll,

eyes painted still, fixed on the table,
branded a symbol of execution,
the smell of metal on metallic blood is never too much,

she would imagine in daydream,
the eighty eight pound blade cracking,
breaking into a million shards flying towards her face,

but she always woke from sleeping
with her eyes wide open, always
watched the next performance, all those cheering behind her,

a mascot will never forget what they represent,
even she who represents death,
and one day she'll get sick of it and try to crawl out the canvas, with

no body to live in, only front legs and a face,
just enough to crawl towards the end,
paws with no claws silent in the gravel, on the wood,

on the cutting board, she's done with everything
with her pancake head on the stool,
she spent forever just reaching, reaching, for the rope.

# late apology

i promise i wasn't trespassing,
to anyone who saw me walk
through your backyard with my backpack
and my face concealed,
i swear.

i know how it looked and i know
how i felt, panting
the air i knew would soon be gone,
bugs crawling up my body, i
didn't care.

i had come too far to think
about the hair i'd left
in the sink and drain, the bed left unmade,
dog waiting for me to return,
my messy room,

it might sound bad,
i might have been sad at the time,
but it became a meticulous plan,
i couldn't have canceled
if i tried.

# painter's tape

peel off the tape on the edge of the paper,
let the paint slide away,
seep into the table where i left myself intertwined
in the wood, trapped under the newspaper,
with it my will to go on,
to choke down prescriptions, and look in their eyes,
finish the painting in progress for years,
old acrylic, wet and watered down by tears, unsatisfied,
removed the tape, the barrier between
self-destruction and hypochondria
and one took over the other.

# halloween costume

walking.
aimless, in my bedsheet ghost disguise,
i forgot to cut holes for my eyes,
but that's okay, i know these one-car-wide roads
like i know my own mind, even when all i see is whiteness;

no protection for my
legs, my barefoot toes burnt on the pavement, wearing down,
i don't swing my arms like a human,
have to pull off this ruse, even when the chafing
of my thighs hurts even worse, i can only walk today;

a car hasn't come by
in thirty minutes, i'm starting to question
where i'm headed, if it's even halloween,
if i'm a friendless, teenage trick-or-treater
or just a lonely kid who ran away from home in a
desperate final attempt to be forgotten;

every step grinds my
bones against each other, tightened lips,
keep going, have to get anywhere other than this,
my head cycling through the same two sentences, tiring
me out, eyelids falling so low, pulling on my crooked hairline,

muscle memory moves
my feet when i fall asleep under the sheet, subconsciously convinced
it's still on my bed at home, instead of tempting gnats
with the scent of my sweat,
breathing slows as though i'm not all alone outside at night,
not drifting further from myself and my life.

# peach

i keep a fire
extinguisher beside me,
i built one just in case i start to cry,
so i can shock myself back into being numb.
my life takes place on
my bedroom floor in the dark,
on my knees, the carpet i bled into too many times,
hoping it would not recirculate,
that it would leave me alone
and dry out;

even when i
close my eyes and hands,
the fire is quieter only for seconds,
the heat only tangible in my lungs, i've
got white marks all up and down my skin,
body like a moldy peach,
picked just after the peak of ripeness,
flammable as could be,
left in my human-sized fridge for years,
the only one of my variety,
unwashed, uneaten.

# rest

you are not affected by my staying in bed,
avoiding all the things that made me cry,
i would rather live like this than die
to put myself through pain.

# plexiglass

ha!
unbreakable glass, that can't be true,
i can't be trapped here when the doors are shut.
i have to know i could run through it if i need to.
i have to be able to escape when the doors lock.
how the blinds open, through twist or pull,
won't prove if the half-assed slab protects us,
whether it ensures safety or traps us in lonely rooms
growing bugs, grass, from pills as unfortunate seeds,

reflection of glass on ceiling tiles,
flowers glittering, though muted, through it,
i can't tell if they're real or painted on the window.
since i started sleeping here, ecosystems formed,
plexiglass sealed us off from the natural world,
enough still water to form colonies of bugs.
they taught us to make our own society, we did, a world of fear,
confused, fighting over stray animals for food,

we become more and more animal ourselves,
normalizing hunting ourselves, each other, convinced
we weren't cannibals because those hunted were "shits."
lord of the flies of the tall, brick,
prison-like building waiting, month after month
after scream after fight, fear in our chests anticipating
nighttime attacks, they could enter our room in silence,
we can't stop it,

they've got a shiv or bat or a hardcover book,
plastic water bottle to the head,
hear the shatter, and think,
was it glass?
a window?
a means of escape? no.
i can laugh at the word,
unbreakable,
but i know.

# ode(?) to my door

you will keep my secrets when i can't,
you will stop the fire from seeping out,
you lock without locking, slam without slamming,
keep out the water, keep out the love,
you're the thing that holds my blood, my flames,
my knives inside, blocks the world from seeing my pig-face,
traps me in this comfortable but terrifying room
where i was born, where i died, where i rest,
i am tired and lost and so, so cold,
but you house my pile of blankets, my shadows and aches,
keep me separated, don't let me ask for help,
you see me in every state, in every way.

# talking about me

i have to keep on,
stay glued to the ceiling,
mechanical,
security camera observes
as they move on from me and my voice,

i hear you talking
about me, my last will and
testament,
recording my final words
to bury with my body, playing on repeat.

if you knew how i felt
before my gravity reversed, what
would you
have done? deliquesce
into the popcorn paint, and fall away?

for your sake, i'll stay a consumer
of your unintended
entertainment,
preserve your spoken tears and
play them back if i get bored,

i hope you miss me less than
i miss you, i can't think i
made a mistake,
i hope my letter satiates in
ways i couldn't have,

i would tell you i love you
if it wouldn't make it worse,
i don't want it to
hurt more than it should,
i'll keep taunting myself, watching,

everything you said to me
before i ended up here is
another piece
of tape on my back, pulling
out my hair as i'm congealing,

on the ceiling still with battery
running out, but you keep talking,
talking about me,
i don't want to miss out on all the
things you never said to my face.

# who am i

"it depends who's asking"
not saying that so you'll tell me who you are, but because it's true
i am not me to everyone, i am everyone but
if you're my family i am a child
because a child needs
it's not that i need love, or attention or food
rather that i need to feel like a child
like there is someone taking care of me
and that comes with guilt and responsibility
i think i'm a disappointment when this is me

if you're my friend then i'm just like you
because i like you
and i want to be liked by you
i am you because you are funny and smart and kind and
being you must mean i'm cool
so i'm a replica
when this is me i feel like there's less pressure to be unique
when this is me i think i'm useless when i leave

but to myself
i am a fraud, i am a loser.
i am a gross balloon of blood, stuck
living under my damp rock in the sewer of mud
that infects my love for myself,
because on my own i don't have to impress, i don't have to be good, i
just have to live on.
"me" to myself is a pawn, a ghost made of scars with a hole in its heart
but this "me" is only real when i'm alone.

# laced up

two strings tied in a bow round my throat, hanged
from the top of the door, cut
into my skin, nails
on my neck, screaming
as i was dying, fallen
onto the ground, kicking, gasping,
head against the wall, against the floor,
defecation.
eyes watching me, after the fact, hours
in the bathroom, cleaning
up the mess i made of myself, crying
at the scar i could barely hide, pretending
that they cared, or even noticed, guilty
of causing pain, hearing
"at least your neck's not
broken," but what about
the rest of me?

# unflavored addiction

disheveled and sunburnt and guilty of
spilling daily pills on the floor,
the dog comes running as if
addicted to things he's never tasted,
i would come running, too, if my mom
dropped something unknown.
i would fold for paradoxes, break the bones
that may or may not exist as cats
in the box of my skin, in the bubble wrap
of pajama pants

in the room i first heard my parents cry.
if no one sees me am i real?
will you feel my death like i would feel
yours, or flower away into soil
and cocaine and decay?
i thought maybe if i was small enough
silent enough, i would snap and stop
complaining about the hot pink stains
i smudged on this face, birthday after birthday.

he survived devouring two doses of medication
i survived a hundred, we both
came back a little bit hooked on the untasted
and intangible, missing places where i
could safely claim i wasn't the problem.
i used to never lie about this
never stumbling over hands holding cures
for artificial illness, seasonal starvation
mystery pills or headspaces—never asked for,
might embrace.

# puddles

fluent in interference,
i seep into skin that doesn't belong to me,
cower in my presence, knowing i am a lie,
too big to stay in my body in peace, in calm,

i have crashed to the ground
too many days to care about the way it hurts,
i've died more times than i have lived,
i've seen more hate than i could give at my lowest,

would have done anything
to capture that disintegrating feeling,
maybe it would let me float, for once,
i could see myself less blurry, see the ground below me,

if i wash away the blood on the pavement,
it doesn't fade, it spreads, contaminates the puddles
filled with me and my regrets, the gore
will dry and leave remains that tell the story of my illness,

please stop praising me, please, it
just makes me fall faster, malnourished and cold,
i'm too old to be aided like this, i can't
see you fail to try and lift me up, i'm too heavy to be saved, just get
inside, i'm scared to hurt you.

# making vows

i take the power vested in me
to bind myself to my dirty towel,
to have and to hold and to keep myself
from being clean, take the space i need away
and spend all our time intertwined,
splatter, squeeze it out, diluted dirt, grey skin residue,
buildup after weeks of laying still

don't judge me for my habits, it's my towel's
fault for failing to dry me off,
i laid out instructions and it slept,
maybe i buy a new one,
but i'm scared it won't know me like this does, it might
be too much to ask, it might become another spectacle, the
unintentional museum of my bath,

even when the dryer breaks in protest, my
hair can't keep dripping onto my clothes
and i have to do something, so there,
there is comfort, and i won't throw it away, because i made a vow.
to have. and to hold. and to decompose together
on the second floor of my parent's house,

we can stare at the holes in the showerhead,
i can be content in being this way,
i don't need to over enunciate the
words i know by heart, they're carved in the miniscule flakes
of my skin and nails
that the fabric knows so well, the softness faded into those sentences,
after all a towel doesn't last forever.

would it be mad if i mistook it for a bathmat,
and gave it the loving task of
flattening under my feet under my
weight that seems like never enough, a
lways too much, is the cruelty great
enough to let this alternate hypothetical hell go back into my dreams?

i hope it likes dandruff, here's my anniversary
gift it's all i have right now, i'm sorry
i can't do more than try to wash my ass and sigh
at every time i smell of mildew asking my partner in crime
what the scent is like
when i know there is no nose, i just have to remember my speech,

there is no power, no lawful wedding, the dress
didn't fit on me anyway, and it was
more of a funeral gown since
i wore it just before i died last year,
i wish i had been wearing what i wanted
and not what it asked of me, even when it unravels i stay,
and keep it close, hoping i didn't make a mistake.

# ambulance

am i a blue light?
i seem to be stocked full of gauze,
alcohol, gloves, and medical knowledge not fit for a kid,
i can tend to your injuries better than most,
replace your brain if you want, so you can stop thinking about it,

if it's blood you need,
i've got plenty, it's just as bright as me, as flashy
as my siren, it clots for your convenience, just thin
enough to drink, i'd give you the rest,
but i might want it later, you're not the only one i treat,

you'll be fine tonight,
my emergency lights will get you home safe,
it's just a matter of time and medication, just a few more minutes
of pain until it goes away, wait, it's almost
over, i'm right here, look at my blank face and get ready to forget,

get ready to be blue,
or red, or white, anything to indicate
i'm not doing my job by the rules, i got too attached to
your big cerulean eyes, too close
to a feeling that we might make it through tomorrow, maybe you're
too much for me to heal.

# on what i share with you

whatever is left of me you can have it
i will fit my body into yours, glass
eyes rolling about, rubber shoes squishing,
squeaking against the wet floor,

would you let me stick my skin to yours,
i think i brought some adhesive
strips, thicker than my blood, stickier that my spit, a
nd perfect for your collarbones,

i'll take your smoke and replace it with
my own, my bones feel perfect
on your floor, rubble blending in with
my wide open greasy pores releasing fire,

i've spent more time in myself than should
have been real, i'd let you snatch the life
right out and let it sink to the wood, feed the dogs,
the scarlet berries we used to eat,

i'll save you a place in my home, where the blankets are
always cold, we can live on body heat and munch
on pretty leaves, as unique as your face on my chest,
use my air wisely, it's all that's left.

# doubt

i wish i could be alone without thinking this much.
everything i do outside this room is wrong, somehow;
i can wring the blood out of my hair, fill
my wounds with alcohol, i can bang my head against the wall but
only feel frustration, never pain in my skull, i don't know
where i lost it,

did i safety pin my lips to my ears for too long? i thought
i was doing right, finally thought the silver was meant to be,
i can dance in a sewer without moving at all,
if the stars could admit that i'm real, and tell me
what to say, maybe i could prove my socks are not the
enemy of my feet,

i will stare at the glass and fight the urge to smash
the mirror and let it cut me up, it seems no matter
how naked i am i could still peel away more,
ogres are like onions; so i slice myself up and cry,
keeping in mind that onions can't socialize or make
mistakes, or fail;

isolating is nice when i'm not disappointing myself.
messing up seventy-five times in one night doesn't
make for good dreams, doesn't make me more real,
i can feel like a little death in a wormhole
that only leads back here, back to sleep trying to dream up
how to be more valuable;

if the clouds in my eyes precipitate they don't go
away, they stay and tutor me in self-destruction,
knowing what is going on but never telling me, seeing
less and less each time i think about the mirror's touch,
the cold, uncomplicated edge of the razors behind it,
my only comfort is glass.

# helium

my head is bigger than my body
a balloon that inflates and floats
and leaks screaming air out the holes in my stomach,
my face has morphed, a metallic bubble of helium,
picks up my body as if it was nothing, takes the control
from my weakened appendages,
i didn't stop the wind from tying my neck in a knot,
from stretching my skin over the air-pump machine
and gilding me, leaving my
brain buried deep in my chest, ecstatic, high
off the static that won't let me lie away my old self,
i am shiny and gold as if the world was on my side
but the world lets me go

# eavesdropping on

visions. they are violent. thirsty canines,
gym guys, bugs. these walls are fused

to my shoulderblades, get stickier when i
sweat or cry. i'd leave behind a sheet of skin

so i might run, scrape away with teeth the
pus beneath, spit it out because my

mouth is the only thing not numb. i can't stand
to kick me when i'm down, so they

plastered me up and drew a spiky smile
on my face. she likes it. maybe i do, maybe i

asked for this, maybe i've listened to bitter
stories until they're clearer than my own.

i think i've already died with my eyes wide open
because all i've done is watch.

# poorly kept

dust can gather,
my hair can fall out of my once anemic head,
my earrings can move from my arm to my lobes
and repeat, repeat without rinsing,

real, authentic
dermis nearly disconnected from the blood that
should be, harboring the sepsis of drab and muddy
thoughts, bedsheets sealing it in like gauze,

sleeping twenty
hours at a time with allergy medicine tying my
limbs to my bed, capsules covering me in a
hot pink mirage, dreaming only in blue,

things that i don't
have the vitality to do without tripping on my own feet,
i can be all talk no action and still be deemed a danger
to a person i don't recognize,

if my bones could
unfreeze without tremors and aches there might
have been a way to rest without dreaming, sleeping as
deeply as i can so eventually i can rise.

# about the author

Chris Taylor (any pronouns) is a young, teen poet from a small, picturesque town in New England, drawing inspiration from the ever-changing world around them—the quiet strength of trees, the bustle of city streets, and the gentle hush of falling snow. Their poetry is rich with metaphor and open to interpretation, inviting readers to find their own meaning in the spaces between the lines. Chris's work has been featured in several online literary journals. They currently live with their parents, twin sibling, and two beloved dogs, finding joy and creativity in the rhythm of family life.

# OUTPOST
## PRESS
AN IMPRINT OF WAYFARER BOOKS

At Wayfarer Books we believe poetry is the language of the earth. We believe words—shaped like rivers through wild places—can change the shape of the world. We publish poets and writers and renegades who stand outside of mainstream culture—poets, essayists, and storytellers whose work might withstand the scrutiny of crows and coyotes, those who are cryptic and floral, the crepuscular, and the queer-at-heart. We are more than just a publisher but a community of writers. Our mission is to produce books that can serve as a compass and map to all wayfarers through wild terrain.

## WAYFARERBOOKS.ORG

www.ingramcontent.com/pod-product-compliance
Lightning Source LLC
Chambersburg PA
CBHW030514130626
46549CB00007B/2998